ELLIOTT CARTER

FIGMENT NO. 2
REMEMBERING MR. IVES

for solo violoncello

www.boosey.com
www.halleonard.com

HENDON MUSIC

DISTRIBUTED BY

HAL•LEONARD®
CORPORATION

7777 W. BLUEMOUND RD. P.O. BOX 13819 MILWAUKEE, WI 53213

First performed December 2, 2001
at Alice Tully Hall, New York City,
by Fred Sherry

Recorded by Fred Sherry
on Bridge Records 9128

Duration: 5 minutes

COMPOSER'S NOTE

Figment No. 2 was composed in the spring of 2001 as a present for the wonderful American cellist Fred Sherry, who with his outstanding instrumental and organizational abilities and his boundless enthusiasms has done so much for music.

This short *Figment* for solo cello recalls fragmentarily bits of the Thoreau movement of the *Concord Sonata* and *Hallowe'en* by my late friend Charles Ives, whose music I have known since 1924 and have loved these works in particular.

—Elliott Carter

AMMERKUNG DES KOMPONISTEN

Figment No. 2 wurde im Frühjahr 2001 als Geschenk für den wunderbaren Cellisten Fred Sherry komponiert, der mit seinen hervorragenden künstlerischen und organisatorischen Fähigkeiten und seinem grenzenlosen Enthusiasmus so viel für die Musik getan hat.

Dieses kurze Stück Figment für Cellosolo erinnert teilweise an den Thoreau-Satz der Concord Sonata und Halloween meines verstorbenen Freundes Charles Ives, dessen Musik mir seit 1924 bekannt war und dessen Werke ich besonders liebte.

—Elliott Carter

NOTE DU COMPOSITEUR

Figment No. 2 a été composé au printemps 2001 comme cadeau pour le merveilleux violoncelliste américain Fred Sherry qui, avec ses remarquables capacités instrumentales et organisationnelles et son enthousiasme sans borne, a tant apporté à la musique.

Ce court *Figment* pour violoncelle solo reprend des fragments du mouvement Thoreau de la *Concord Sonata* et de *Hallowe'en* de feu mon ami Charles Ives, dont je connais la musique depuis 1924, ces morceaux faisant partie de mes favoris.

—Elliott Carter

for Fred Sherry

FIGMENT NO. 2
REMEMBERING MR. IVES

Elliott Carter
(2001)

M-051-10442-0

Printed in U.S.A.

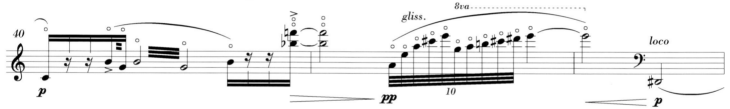

CHAMBER MUSIC OF
ELLIOTT CARTER

TRIPLE DUO (1983)   20'
for flute (doubling piccolo), clarinet (doubling E♭ and bass clarinets), percussion, piano, violin, and cello

CHANGES (1983)   7'
for guitar

CANON FOR 4 (1984)   4'
"Homage to William"
for flute, bass clarinet, violin and cello

RICONOSCENZA PER GOFFREDO PETRASSI (1984)   4'
for solo violin

ESPRIT RUDE / ESPRIT DOUX (1984)   4'
pour Pierre Boulez
for flute and B♭ clarinet

STRING QUARTET NO. 4 (1986)   24'

ENCHANTED PRELUDES (1988)   6'
for flute and cello

BIRTHDAY FLOURISH (1988)   1'
for five trumpets or brass quintet

CON LEGGEREZZA PENSOSA (1990)   5'
Omaggio a Italo Calvino
for B♭ clarinet, violin, and cello

SCRIVO IN VENTO (1991)   5'
for solo flute

QUINTET (1991)   20'
for piano and winds

TRILOGY (1992)   17'
    Bariolage *for solo harp*   7'
    Inner Song *for solo oboe*   5'
    Immer Neu *for oboe and harp*   5'

GRA (1993)   4'
for solo B♭ clarinet

GRA (1993)   4'
transcribed for trombone by Benny Sluchin

TWO FIGMENTS
for solo cello
    No. 1 (1994)   5'
    No. 2 – Remembering Mr. Ives (2001)   3'

TWO FRAGMENTS
for string quartet
    No. 1 – in memoriam David Huntley (1994)   4'
    No. 2 (1999)   3'

ESPRIT RUDE / ESPRIT DOUX II (1994)   5'
for flute, clarinet and marimba

OF CHALLENGE AND OF LOVE (1995)   25'
five poems of John Hollander
for soprano and piano

STRING QUARTET NO. 5 (1995)   20'

A 6 LETTER LETTER (1996)   3'
for solo English horn

QUINTET (1997)   10'
for piano and string quartet

LUIMEN (1997)   12'
for trumpet, trombone, mandolin, guitar, harp, and vibraphone

SHARD (1997)   3'
for solo guitar

TEMPO E TEMPI (1998)   15'
for soprano, violin, English horn, and bass clarinet

FRAGMENT NO. 2 (1999)   3'
for string quartet

TWO DIVERSIONS (1999)   8'
for solo piano

RETROUVAILLES (2000)   3'
for solo piano

4 LAUDS (1984-2000)   11'
for solo violin
    Statement – Remembering Aaron (1999)   3'
    Riconoscenza per Goffredo Petrassi (1984)   4'
    Rhapsodic Musings (2000)   2'
    Fantasy – Remembering Roger (1999)   3'

OBOE QUARTET (2001)   17'
for oboe, violin, viola, and cello

HIYOKU (2001)   4'
for two clarinets

STEEP STEPS (2001)   3'
for bass clarinet

AU QUAI (2002)   3'
for bassoon and viola

RETRACING (2002)   3'
for solo bassoon

CALL (2003)   1'
for two trumpets and horn

INTERMITTENCES (2005)   6'
for solo piano

M-051-10442-0

U.S. $14.99

HENDON MUSIC

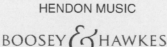

ISBN 978-1-4234-1034-8

BOOSEY & HAWKES

AN IMAGEM COMPANY

DISTRIBUTED BY
Hal•Leonard®

8-84088-05453-3

8 84088 05453 3

HL48019131

9 781423 410348

51499

The Organic Music of

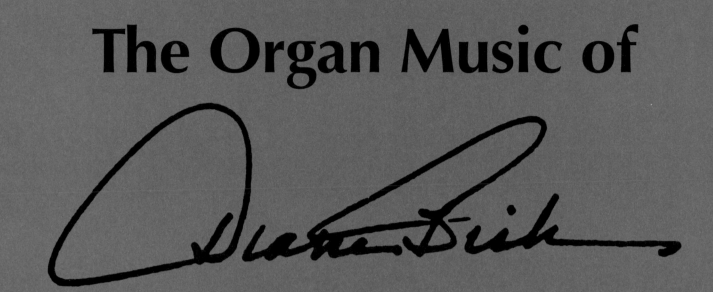

ALL CREATURES OF OUR GOD AND KING

Fred Bock Music Company

EXCLUSIVELY DISTRIBUTED BY
HAL•LEONARD

commissioned by
The Nebraska Music Teachers Association
Omaha, Nebraska AGO Chapter
Lincoln, Nebraska AGO Chapter

Introduction, Theme & Variations on
"ALL CREATURES OF OUR GOD AND KING"

Introduction

Geistliche Kirchengesäng
Arranged by DIANE BISH

Sw. Foundations, Reeds 16, 8, 4; Sw. to Ch. 8, 4
Gt. Solo Trumpet 8
Ch. Foundations, Mixtures, Reeds
Ped. Foundations 16, 8; Bombard 16, 8

Majestic ♩ = 66

BGK1036